Fabulous Fashions of the 1950s Coloring Book

Ming-Ju Sun

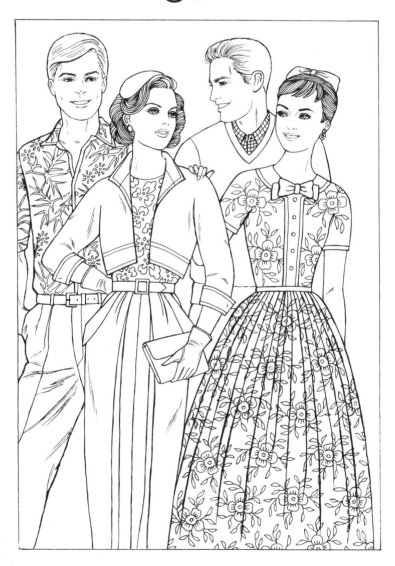

DOVER PUBLICATIONS, INC.
Mineola, New York

The post-World War II period in American history was a time of optimism and growth. From tailored to playful, fashions showed a range of styles. In these beautifully detailed coloring pages by artist Ming-Ju Sun, you'll find an array of Fifties fashions and fads: full pleated skirts, including the iconic "poodle"; floral patterns; ponytails and neatly groomed men's hairstyles; menswear such as car coats, plaid pants and shirts, and casual pullovers; clutch-style handbags; belted waistlines; bolero jackets; and even hula hoops! The unbacked plates allow you to use any coloring media you like, and the perforated pages make displaying your finished work easy. Enjoy coloring these "blast from the past" fashions!

Bibliographical Note
Fabulous Fashions of the 1950s is a new work,
first published by Dover Publications, Inc., in 2016.

International Standard Book Number
ISBN-13: 978-0-486-79906-3
ISBN-10: 0-486-79906-9

Manufactured in the United States by LSC Communications
79906907   2016
www.doverpublications.com

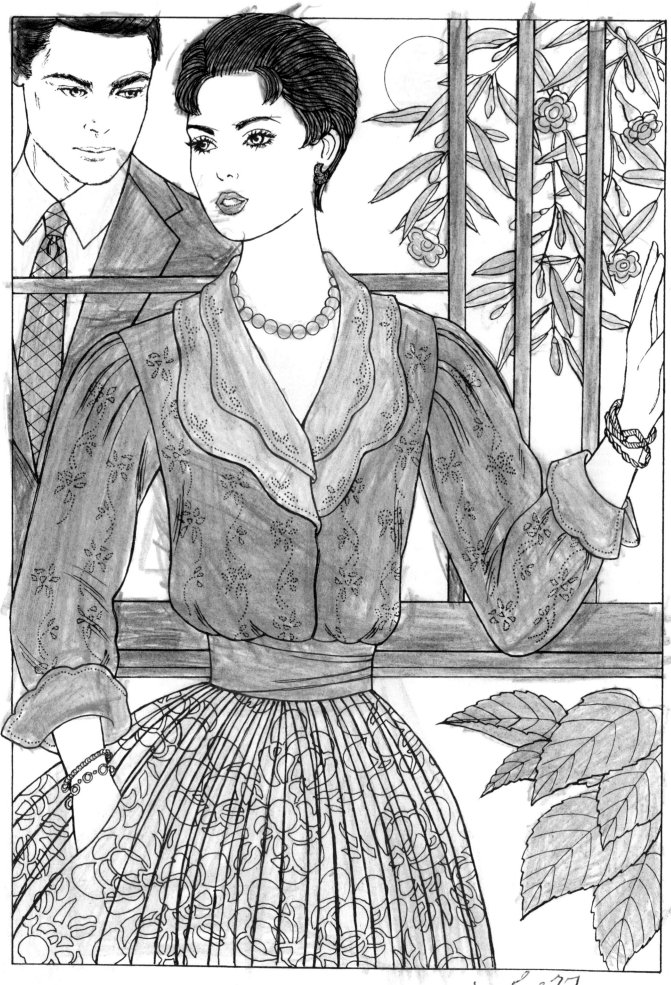

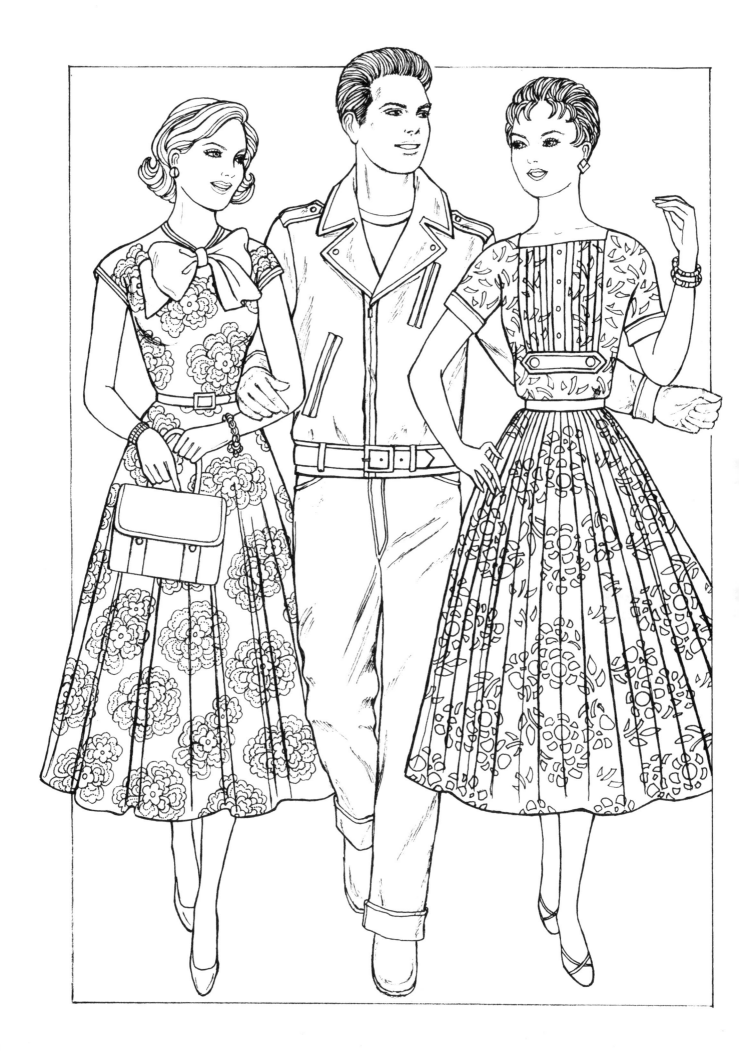

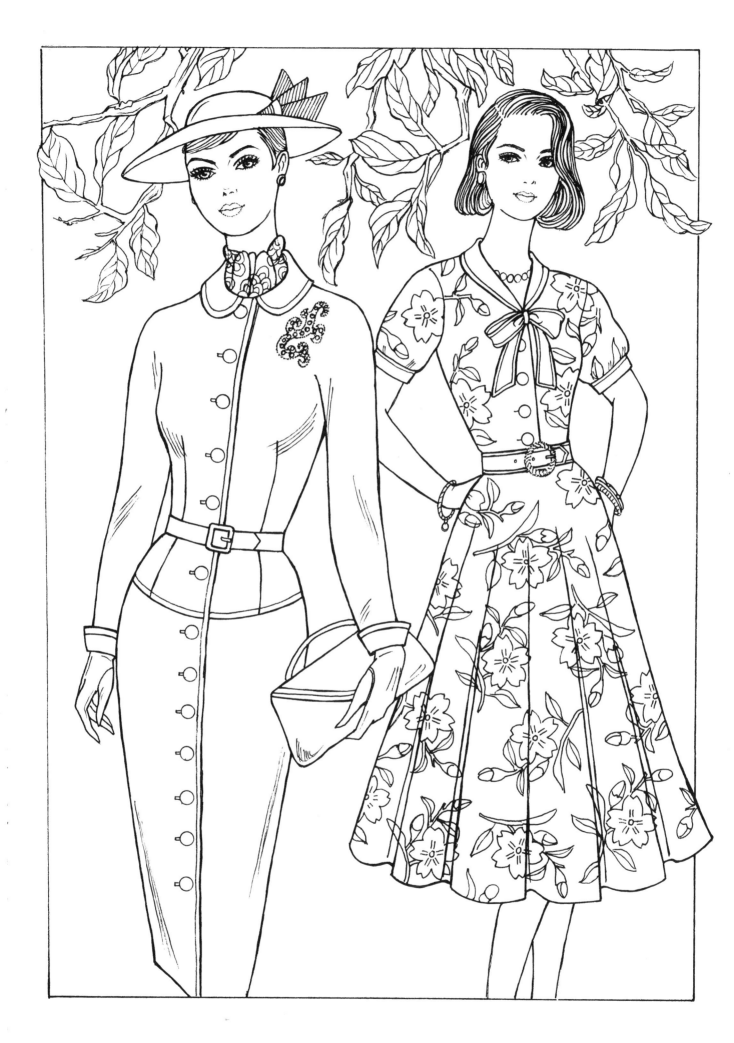

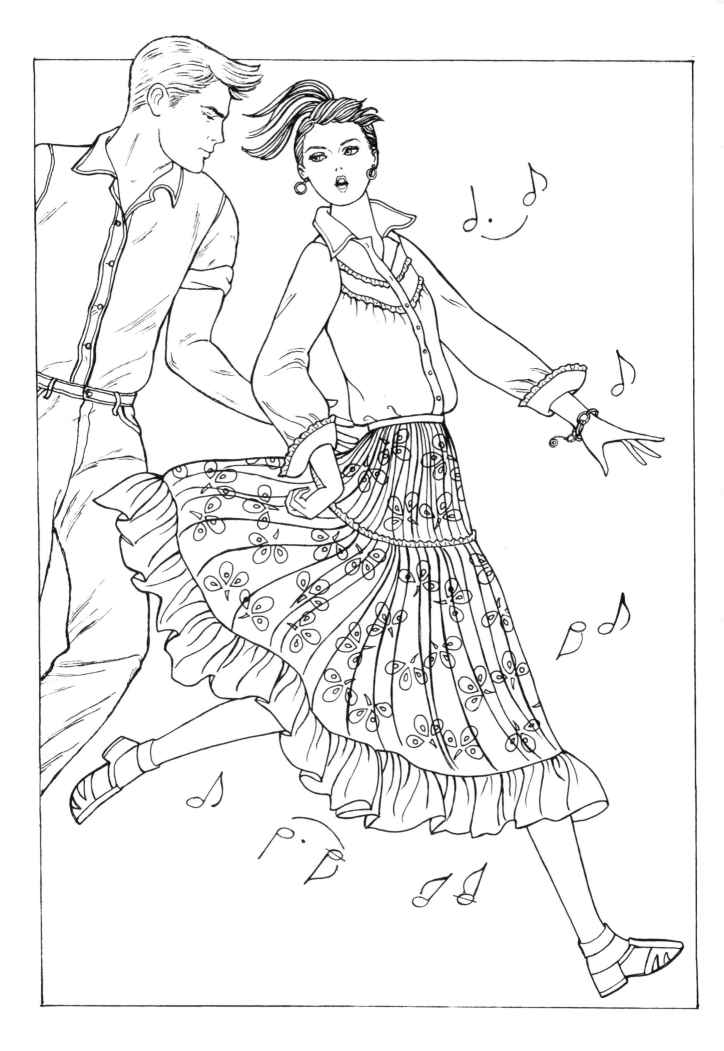

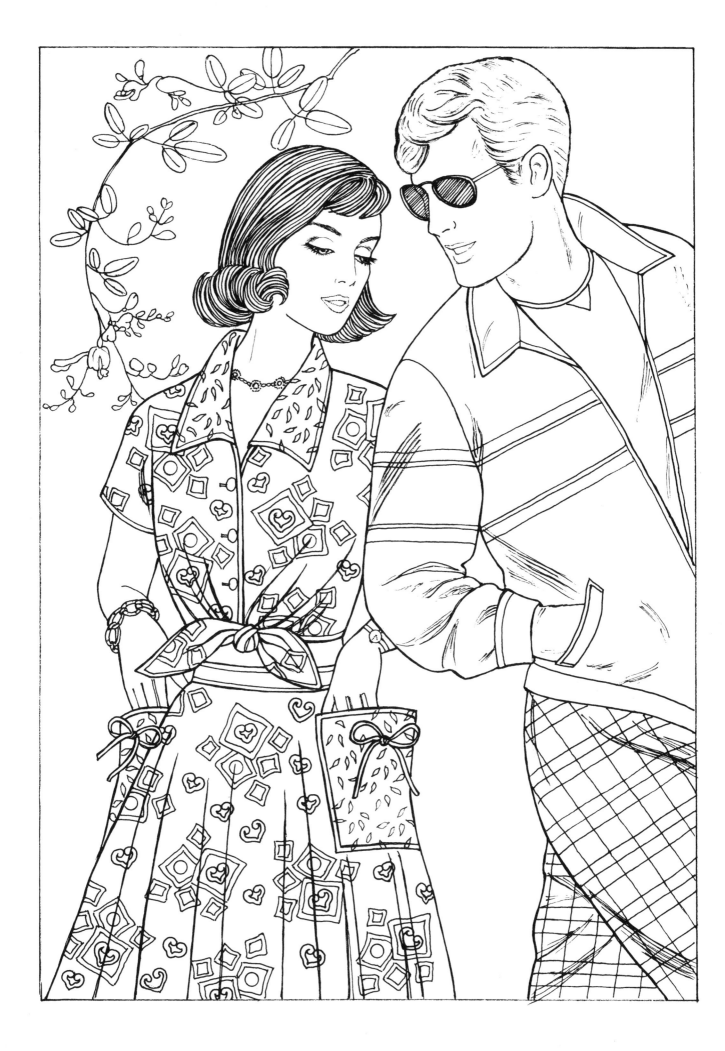

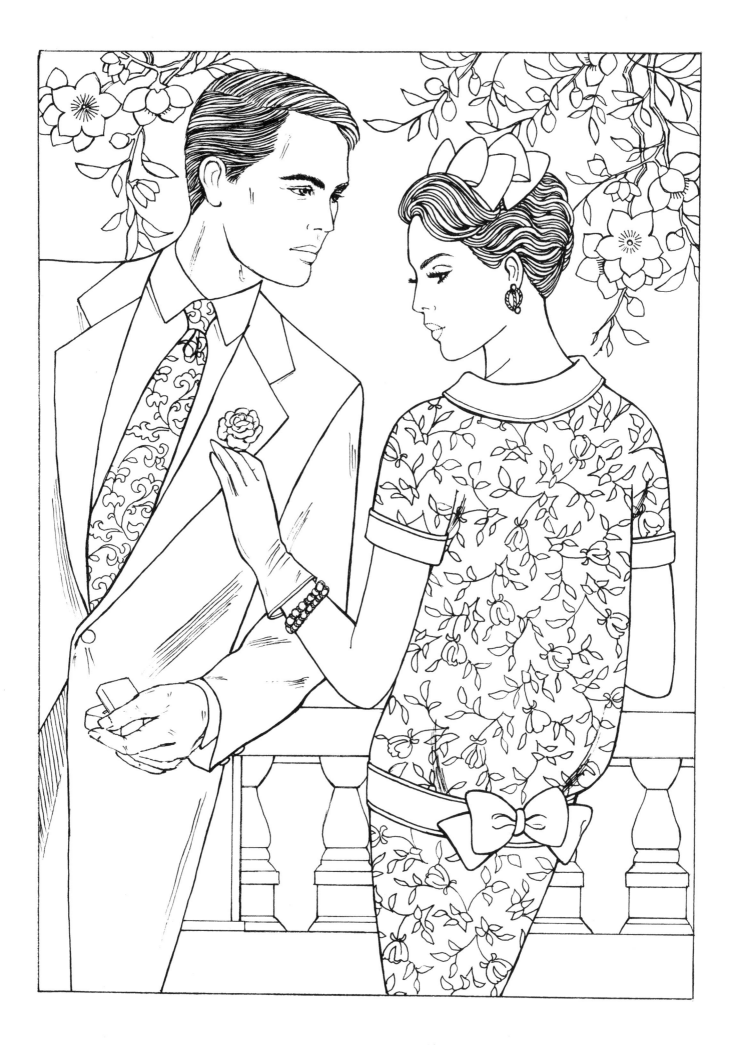

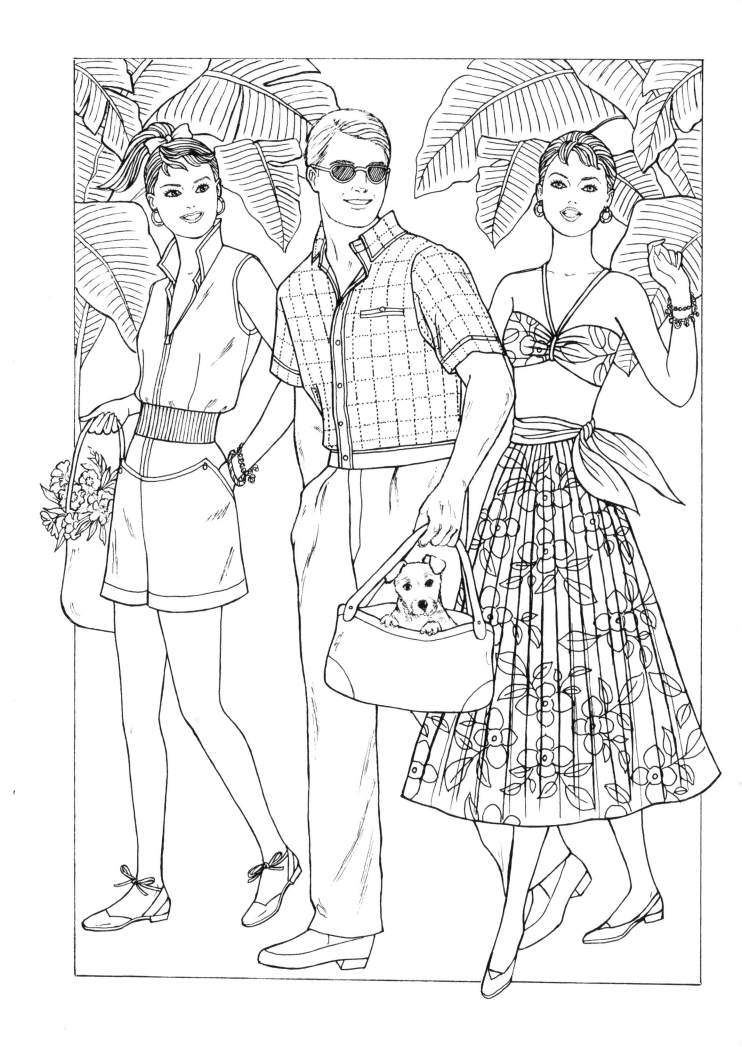

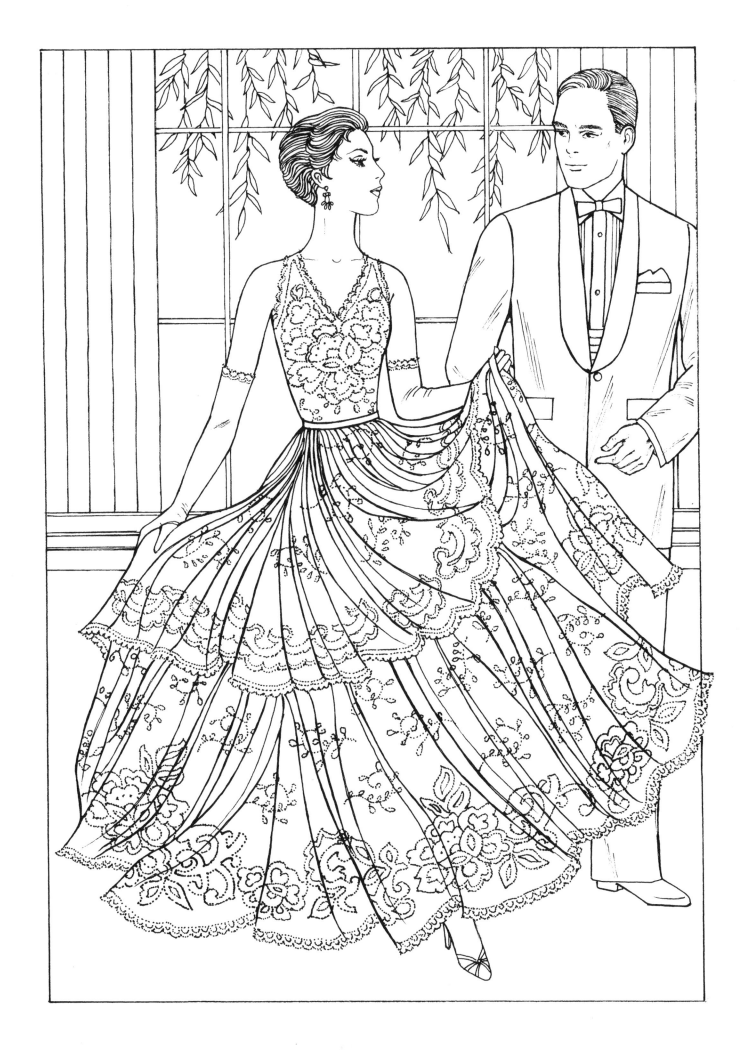

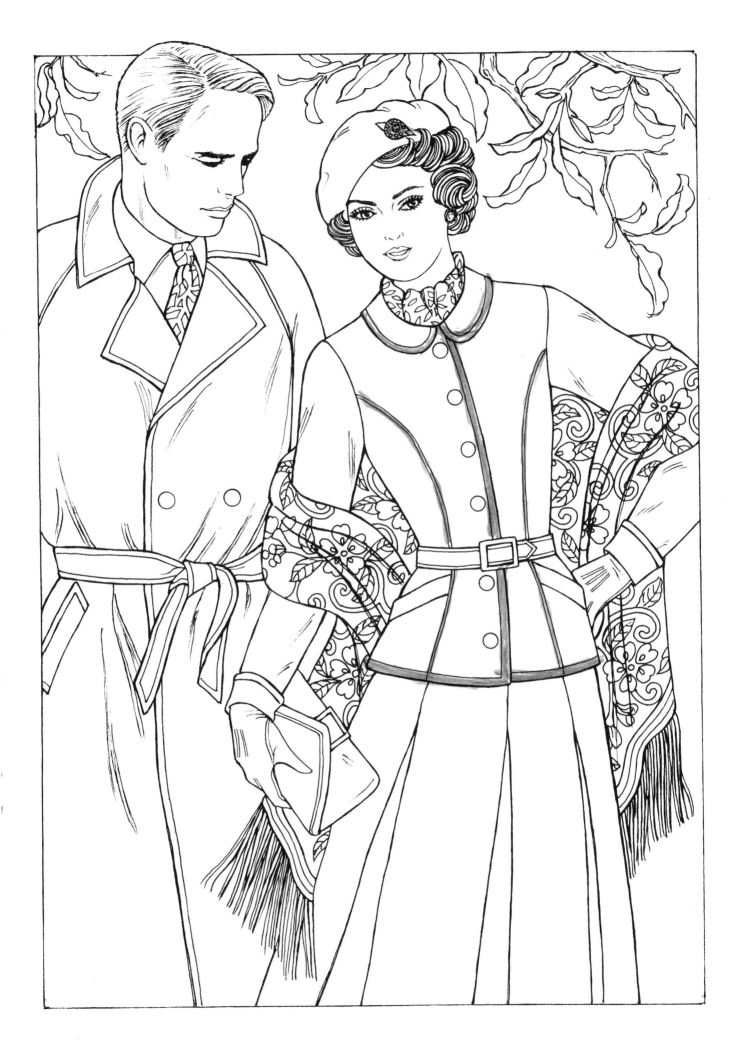

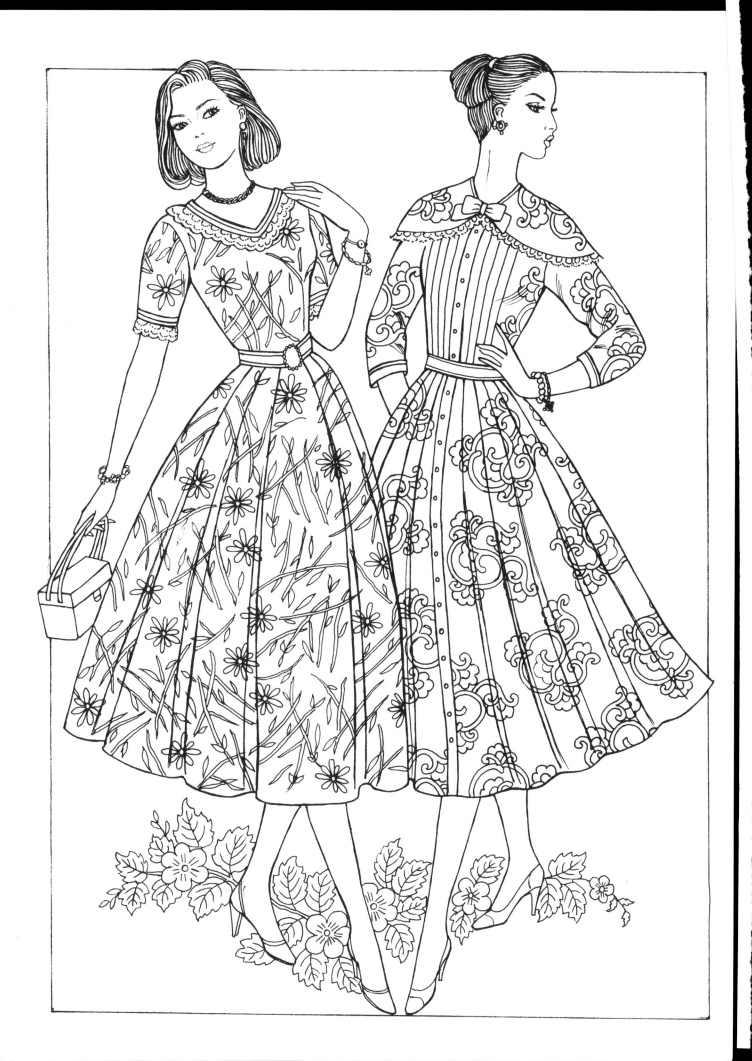

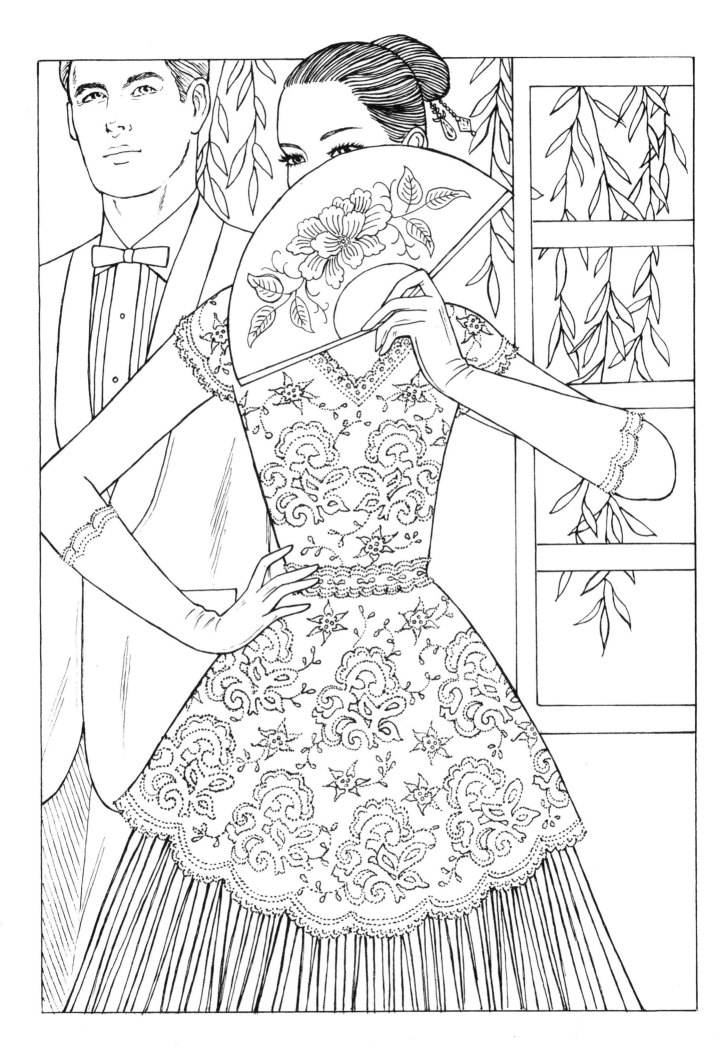

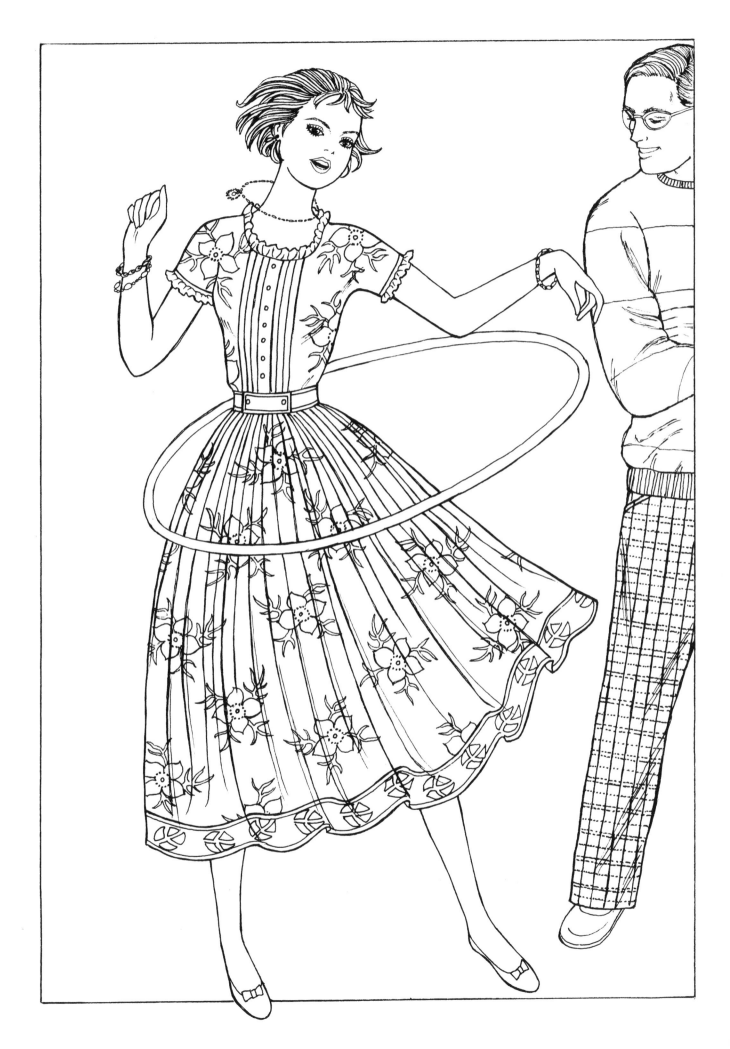

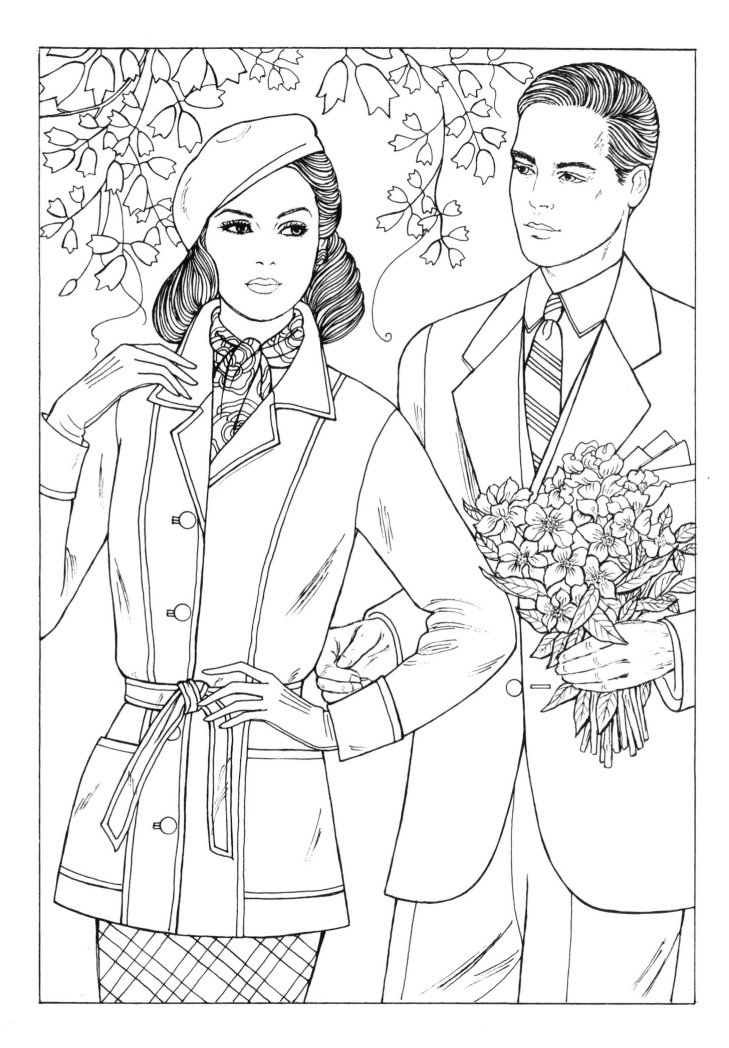

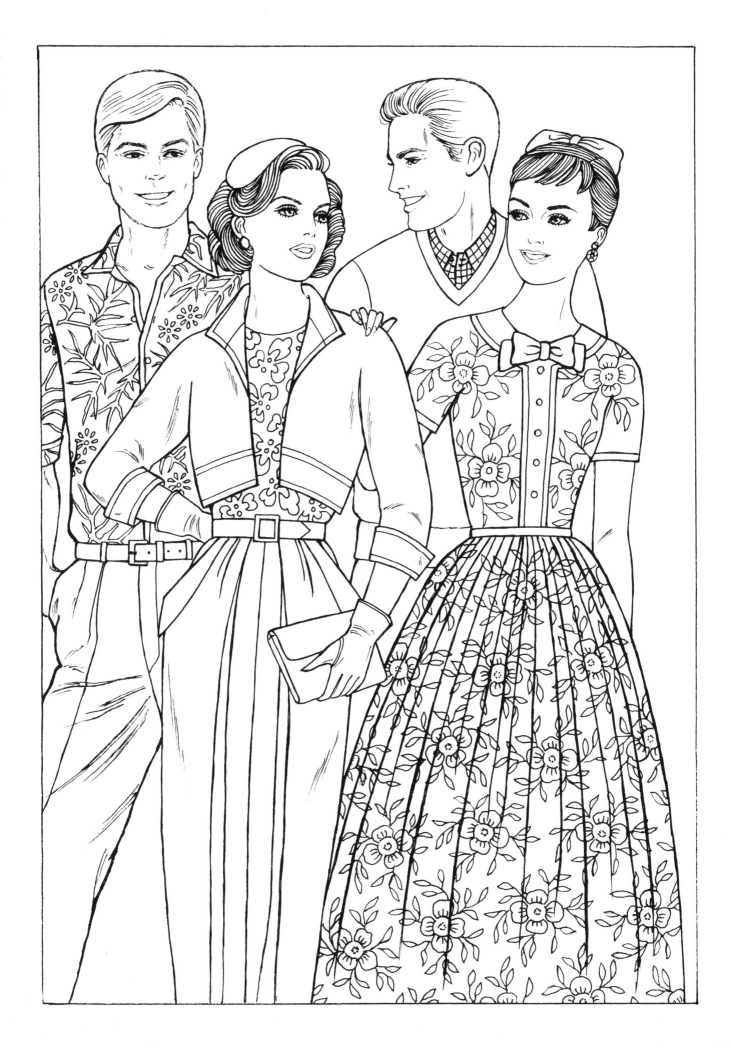

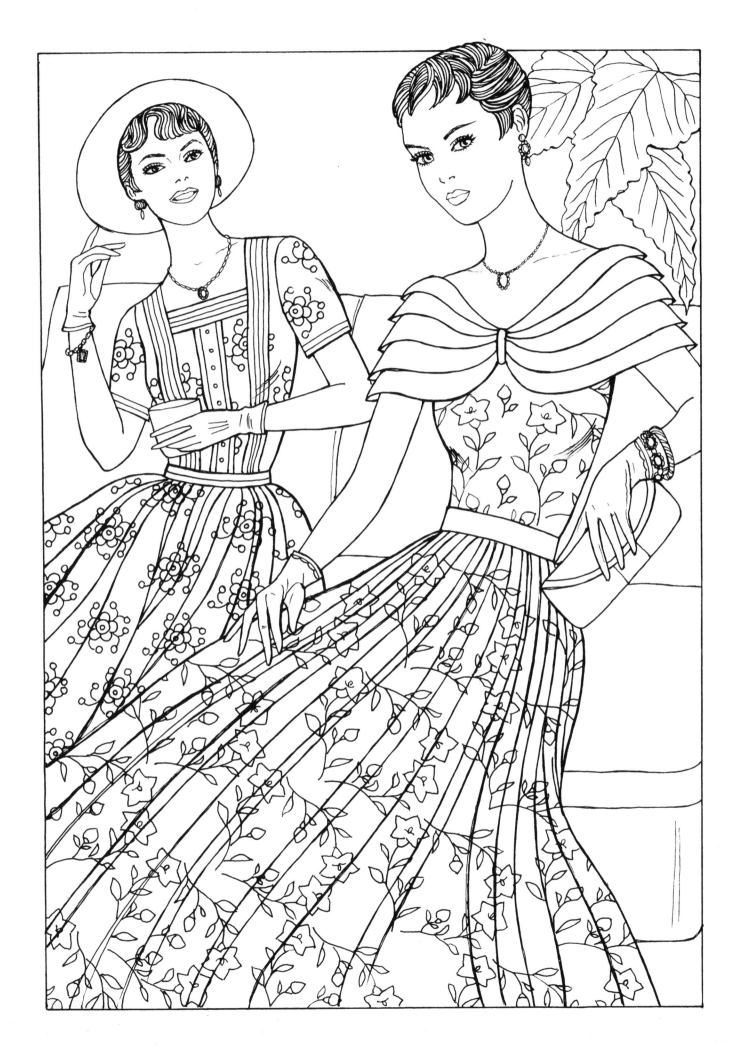

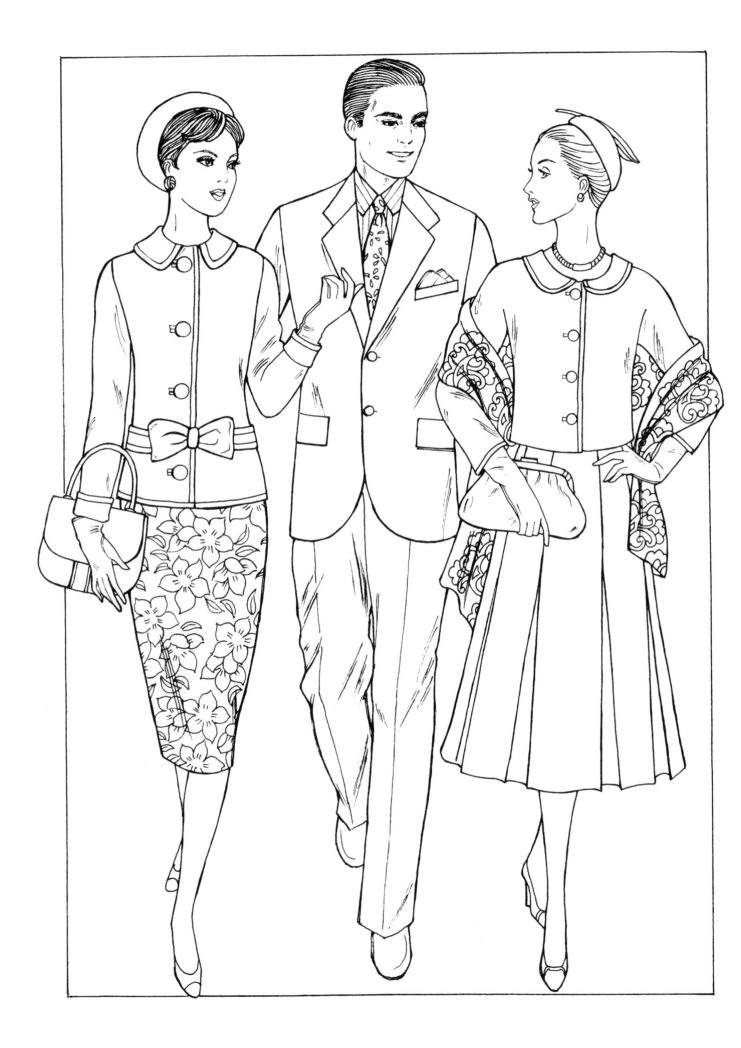

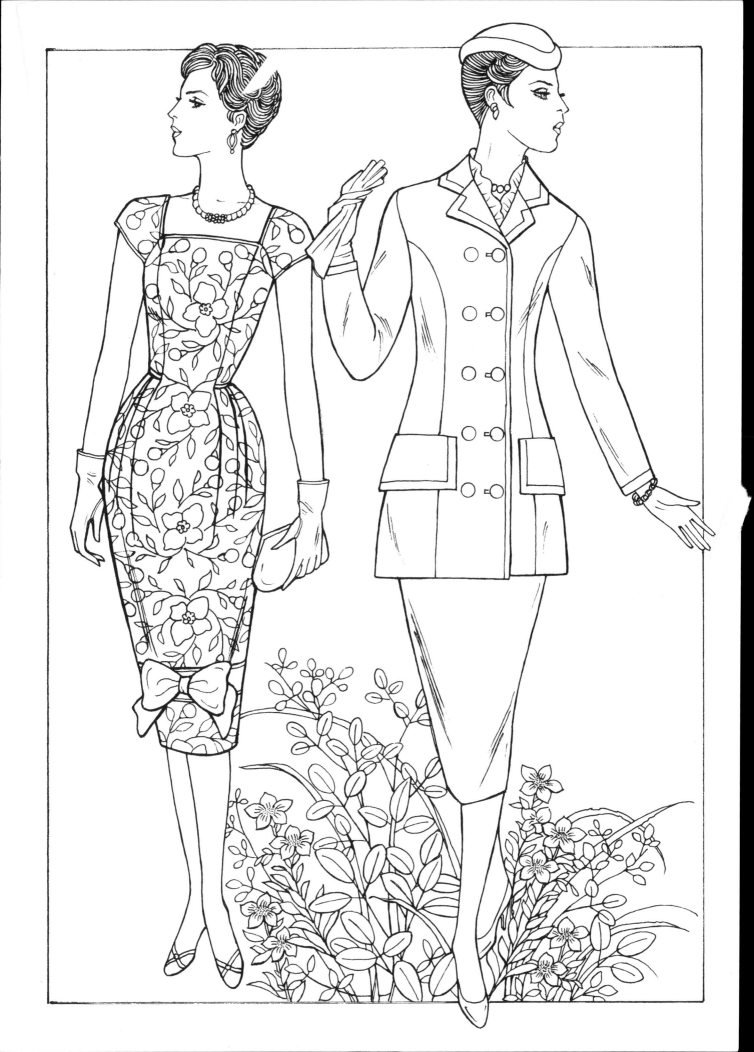

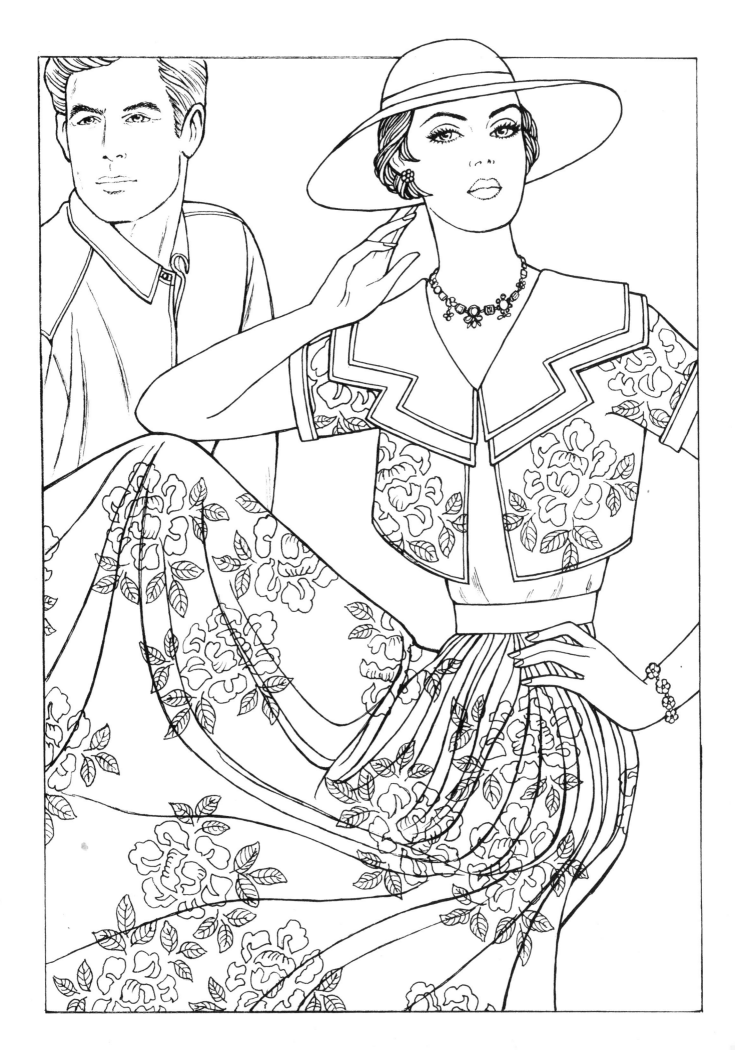

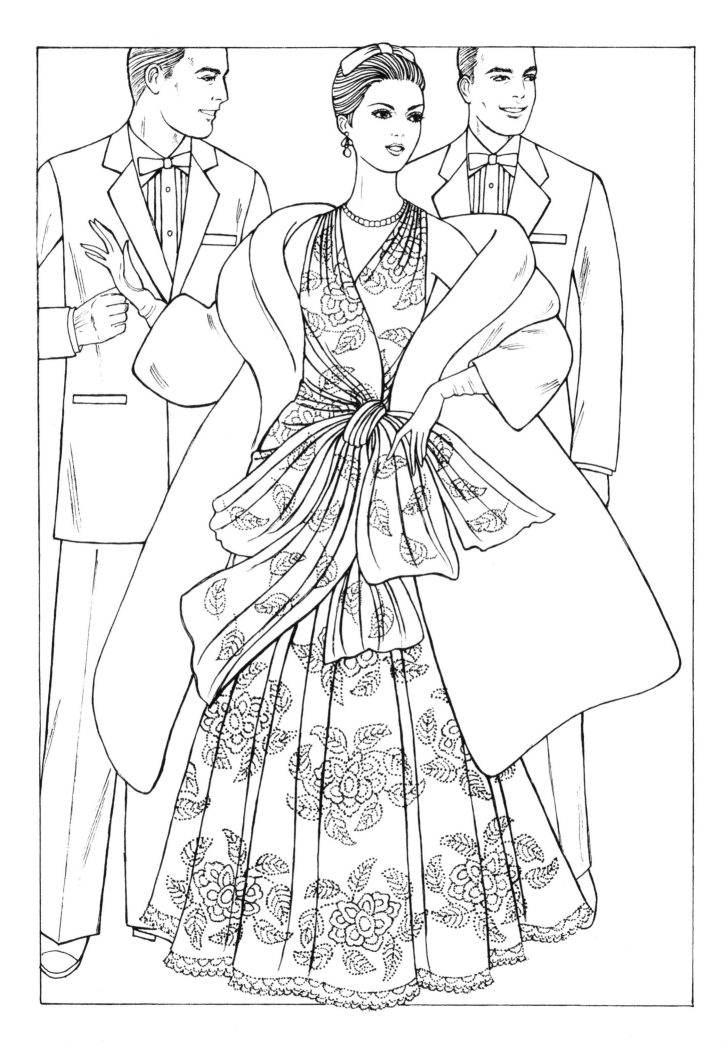

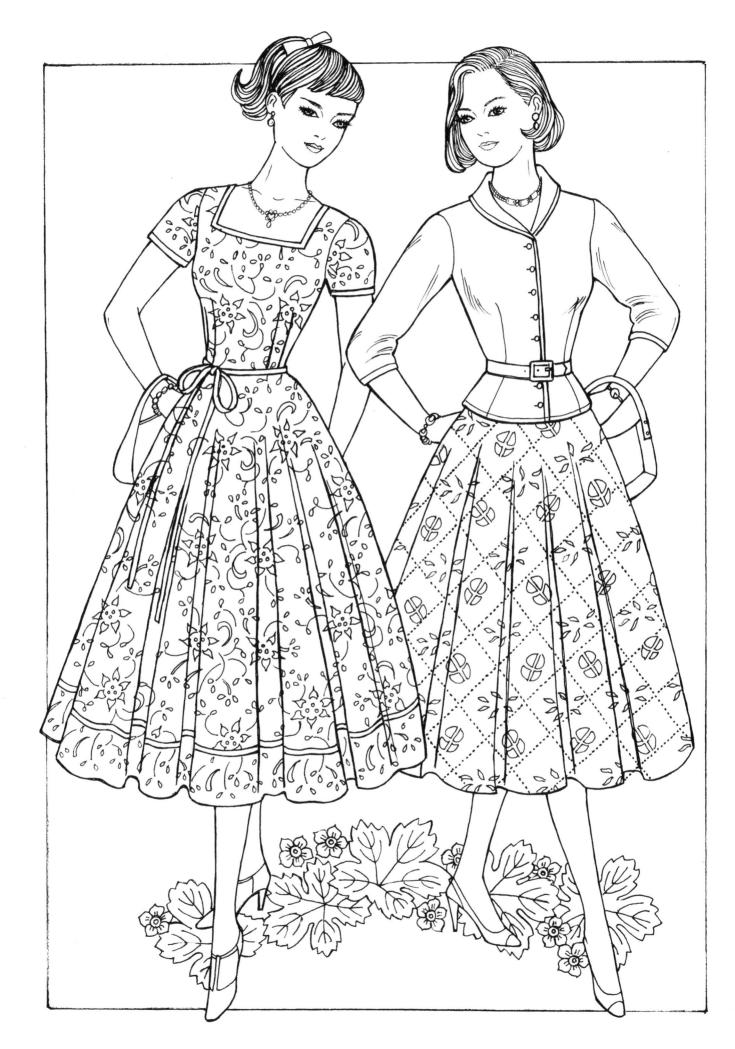

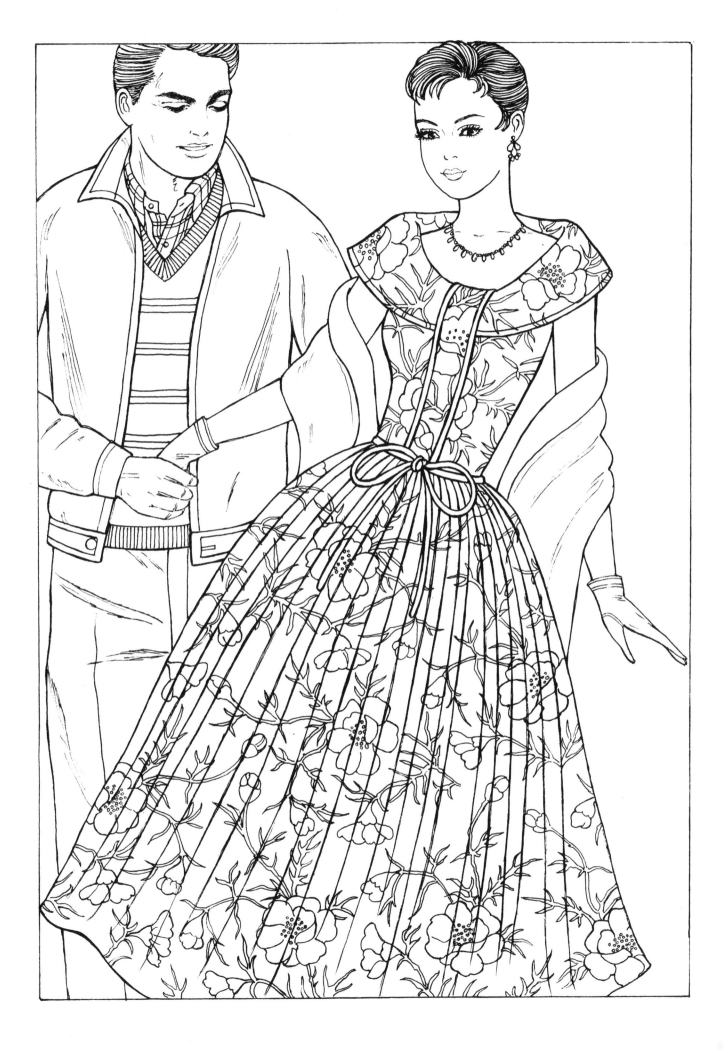

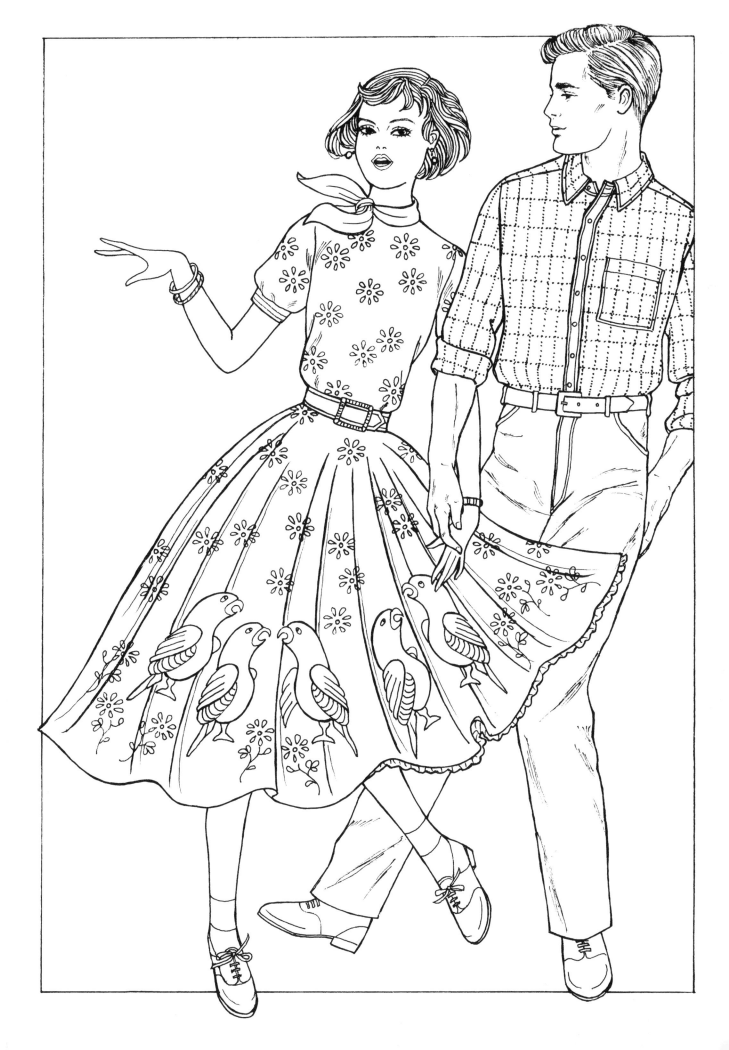

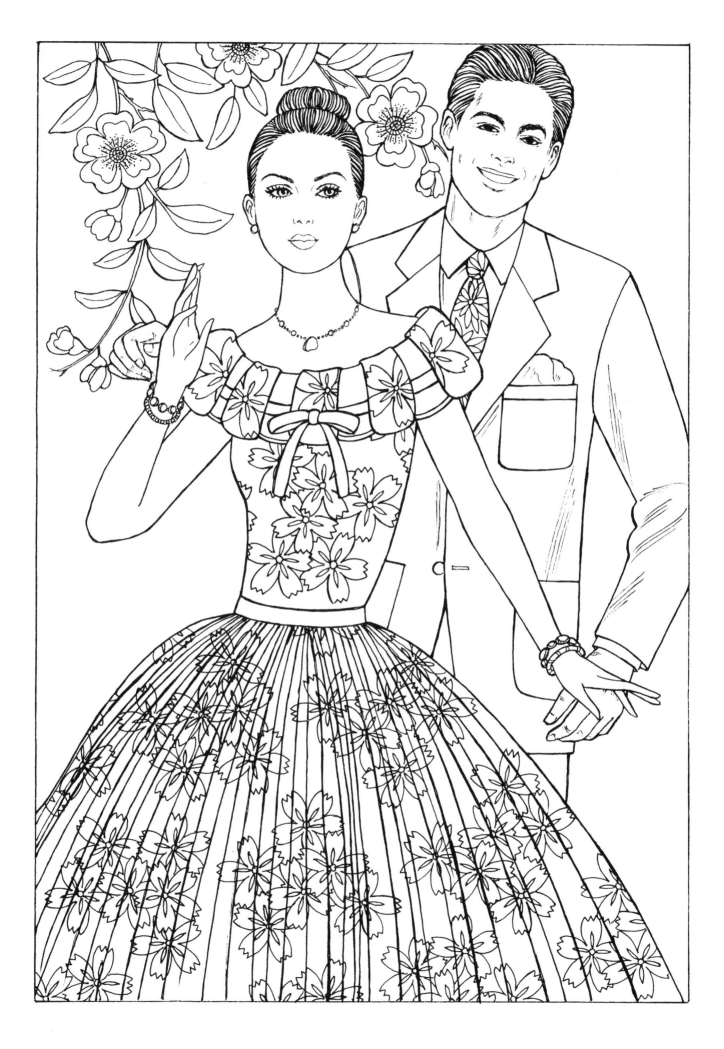

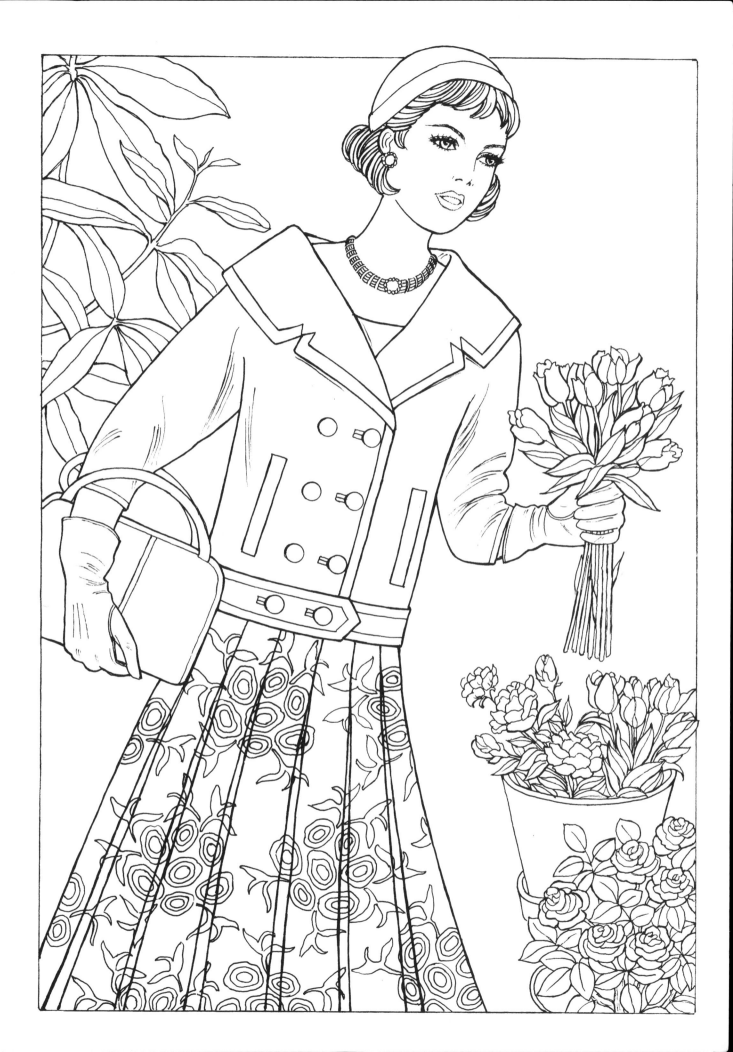